BABY GAMES
AND
LULLABIES

SELECTED BY SALLY EMERSON
ILLUSTRATED BY MOIRA & COLIN MACLEAN

Kingfisher Books

Kingfisher Books, Grisewood & Dempsey Ltd,
Elsley House, 24–30 Great Titchfield Street, London W1P 7AD

First published in 1992 by Kingfisher Books.
10 9 8 7 6 5 4 3
The material in this edition was previously published by Kingfisher Books in
The Kingfisher Nursery Treasury (1988)
and *The Kingfisher Nursery Songbook* (1991).

British Library Cataloguing-in-Publication Data
A catalogue record for this book is available from the British Library

ISBN 0 86272 887 8

Phototypeset by Southern Positives and Negatives (SPAN), Lingfield, Surrey
Printed and bound in Spain

CONTENTS

1

Here sits Farmer Giles,
Touch his forehead.

2

Here sit his two men,
Touch his eyes.

3

Here sits the cockadoodle,
Touch his nose.

4

Here sits the hen,
Touch his lips.

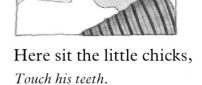
5

Here sit the little chicks,
Touch his teeth.

6

Here they run in,
Chin chopper,
Chin chopper,
Chin, chin, chin.
Tickle his chin.

1

Knock at the door,
Tap her forehead.

2

Ring the bell,
Pull her hair gently.

3

Lift the latch,
Pinch her nose gently.

Eye winker,
Tom tinker,
Nose smeller,

4

And walk in.
Tap your fingers on her lips.

Mouth eater,
Chin chopper,
Guzzlewopper.

5

*Hands back to back,
intertwine fingers.*

Here are the lady's knives and forks,

Turn hands over.

Here's the lady's table,

Raise index fingers.

Here's the lady's looking-glass,

*Raise little fingers
and rock.*

And here's the baby's cradle.
Rock-rock, rock-rock, rock.

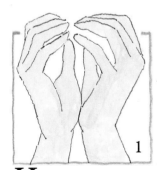   

Here is a ball
for baby,
Big and soft
and round.

Here is a baby's
hammer,
See how it can
pound.

Here is a baby's
trumpet,
Tootle tootle
toot.

Here is the way
my baby
Plays peek-a-boo,
Boo!

Can you keep a secret?
I wonder if you can.
Don't laugh and don't cry
While it tickles in your hand.

1

Two little dicky birds,
Sitting on a wall,

2

One named Peter,
One named Paul.

3

Fly away, Peter!

4

Fly away, Paul!

5

Come back, Peter!
Come back, Paul!

1

J ack-in-the-box jumps UP
like this,

Swing him up high.

2

He makes me laugh when he
waggles his head,

Shake him gently.

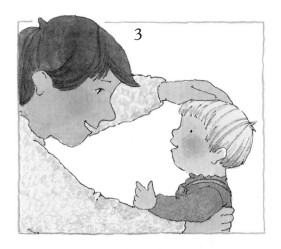

3

I gently press him
down again,

Lower him down.

4

But Jack-in-the-box
jumps UP instead.

Swing him up again.

W hat shall we do with
a lazy Katie?
What shall we do with
a lazy Katie?
What shall we do with
a lazy Katie,
Early in the morning?

Roll her on the bed and
tickle her all over,
Roll her on the bed and
tickle her all over,
Roll her on the bed and
tickle her all over,
Early in the morning.

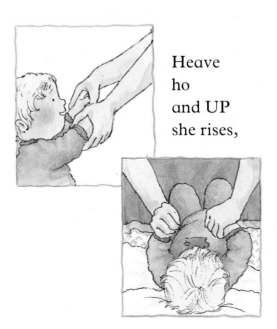

Heave
ho
and UP
she rises,

Heave ho and UP she rises,
Heave ho and UP she rises,
Early in the morning.

♫ *Sing to the tune of "What shall we
do with the drunken sailor?"*

Tinga layo! Come,
little donkey, come.
Tinga layo! Come,
little donkey, come.

Me donkey buck,
Me donkey leap,
Me donkey kick,
wid him two hind feet.

Repeat this verse.

Tinga layo! Come,
little donkey, come.
Tinga layo! Come,
little donkey, come.

*Trot your baby on your knees
or hold him in your arms; lift
him forward at BUCK, up at
LEAP, and backwards at KICK.*

Rock, rock, rock your boat,
Gently down the stream,
Merrily, merrily, merrily, merrily,
Life is but a dream.

This is the way the ladies ride,
Nimble nim, nimble nim, nimble nim;

This is the way the gentlemen ride,
Gallop a trot! Gallop a trot! Gallop a trot!

This is the way the farmers ride,
Jiggety jog, jiggety jog, jiggety jog;

This is the way the butcher boy rides,
Tripperty trot, tripperty trot, tripperty trot,

Till he falls in a ditch with a flipperty,
Flipperty, flop, flop, FLOP!

Sit your child on your knees and bounce her up and down, mimicking the rhythm of the different rides.

End by suddenly dropping the child between your knees. Babies can be bounced or rocked in your arms.

Tom Thumbkin
Willie Wilkin,
Long Daniel,
Betty Bodkin,
And Little Jack-a-Dandy

This little cow eats grass,
This little cow eats hay,
This little cow looks over
    the hedge,
This little cow runs away.
And this BIG cow does
    nothing at all
But lie in the fields all day!
We'll chase her.
    And chase her.
        And chase her!

*A finger-counting rhyme, starting at the
little finger. End by pouncing on the thumb.*

Round and round the garden
Like a teddy bear.
One step, two step,
Tickle you under there!

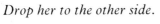

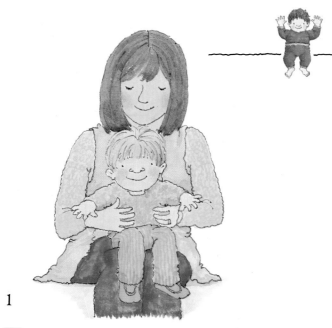

1

2

Father and Mother and Uncle John
Went to market, one by one.

Jog the baby gently.

Father fell off!

Drop her to one side.

3

4

Mother fell off!

Drop her to the other side.

But Uncle John went on, and on,
And on, and on and on.

Now jog faster and faster.

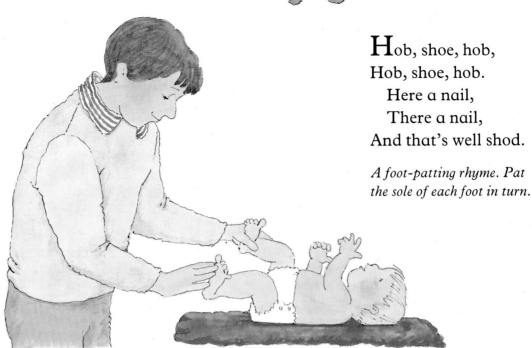

Hob, shoe, hob,
Hob, shoe, hob.
　　Here a nail,
　　There a nail,
And that's well shod.

*A foot-patting rhyme. Pat
the sole of each foot in turn.*

Leg over leg,
As the dog goes to Dover,
When he comes to a wall,
Jump! He goes over!

*Sit the baby in your lap with his back
to you. Cross and uncross his legs in time
to the first three lines. At JUMP lift both
legs up so that he topples back into you.*

15

Jelly on the plate,
Jelly on the plate,
Wibble wobble,
Wibble wobble,
Jelly on the plate.

Wobble from side to side.

Sweeties in the jar,
Sweeties in the jar,
Shake them up,
Shake them up,
Sweeties in the jar.

Shake up and down.

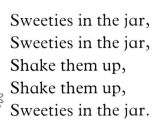

Fire on the floor,
Fire on the floor,
Stamp it out,
Stamp it out,
Fire on the floor.

Bounce to the ground and up.

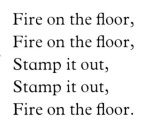

Candles on the cake,
Candles on the cake,
Blow them out,
Blow them out,
Puff puff puff.

Blow each other gently.

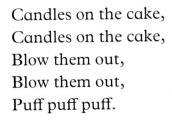

A bouncing rhyme.

Dance to your daddy,
  My little babby
Dance to your daddy,
  My little lamb.

You shall have a fishy,
  In a little dishy,
You shall have a fishy,
  When the boat comes in.

Rigadoon, rigadoon,
Now let him fly,
Sit him on father's foot,
Jump him up high.

*Cross your legs and sit the
baby on your crossed ankle.
Swing up and down.*

This little pig went to market,
This little pig stayed at home,
This little pig had roast beef,
This little pig had none,
And this little pig cried:
Wee-wee-wee-wee-wee-wee,
All the way home!

*An old favourite – count from big to little
toe and end with a tickle.*

1 This pig got into the barn,

Starts at the big toe.

2 This ate all the corn,

3 This said he wasn't well,

4 This said he'd go and tell,

5 And this said: Squeak! squeak! squeak! I can't get over the barn door sill.

Wee Wiggie,
Poke Piggie,
Tom Whistle,
John Gristle
and old BIG GOBBLE,
  gobble, gobble!

A toe-counting rhyme. Start with the little toe and end by seizing the big toe and pretending to gobble it up.

Twinkle, twinkle, little star,
How I wonder what you are!
Up above the world so high,
Like a diamond in the sky.

Then the traveller in the dark
Thanks you for your tiny spark,
He could not see which way to go,
If you did not twinkle so.

In the dark blue sky you keep,
And often through my curtains peep,
For you never shut your eye,
Till the sun is in the sky.

As your bright and tiny spark
Lights the traveller in the dark,
Though I know not what you are,
Twinkle, twinkle, little star.

Star light, star bright,
First star I see tonight,
I wish I may, I wish I might,
Have the wish I wish tonight.

Hush-a-bye, don't
  you cry,
Go to sleepy,
  little baby.

When you wake, you
  shall have a cake
And all the pretty
  little horses.

Blacks and bays,
  dapples and greys,
Coach and six
  white horses.

Hush thee, my babby,
  Lie still with thy daddy,
Thy mammy has gone to the mill,
  To get some meal
  To bake a cake,
So pray, my dear babby, lie still.

The Man in the Moon looked
  out of the moon
Looked out of the moon
  and said:
'Tis time for all children
  on the earth
To think about going to bed!

Wee Willie Winkie runs through the town,
Upstairs and downstairs in his nightgown,
Rapping at the window, crying through the lock:
Are all the children in their beds, it's past eight o'clock?

Niddledy, noddledy,
To and fro.
Tired and sleepy,
To bed we go.

Jump into bed,
Switch out the light,
Head on the pillow,
Shut your eyes tight.

Lie abed,
Sleepy head,
Shut up eyes, bo-peep;
Till day-break
Never wake;
Baby sleep.

Hush, little baby, don't say a word,
Papa's gonna buy you a mocking bird.

If that mocking bird won't sing,
Papa's gonna buy you a diamond ring.

If the diamond ring turns to brass,
Papa's gonna buy you a looking glass.

If that looking glass gets broke,
Papa's gonna buy you a billy goat.

If that billy goat won't pull,
Papa's gonna buy you a cart and a bull.

If that cart and bull turn over,
Papa's gonna buy you a dog named Rover.

If that dog named Rover won't bark,
Papa's gonna buy you a horse and cart.

If that horse and cart fall down,
You'll still be the sweetest baby in town.

Hush-a-bye baby
On the tree top,
When the wind blows,
The cradle will rock;
When the bough breaks,
The cradle will fall;
Down will come baby,
Cradle and all.

Bye low, bye low,
Baby's in the cradle sleeping;
Tip toe, tip toe,
Still as pussy slyly creeping;
Bye low, bye low,
Rock the cradle, baby's waking;
Hush, my baby, oh!

Sleepy time has come
    for my baby,
Baby now is going to sleep;
Kiss Mama good night and
    we'll turn out the light,
While I tuck you in beneath
    your covers tight;
Sleepy time has come
    for my baby,
Baby now is going to sleep.

Golden Slumbers

Golden slumbers kiss your eyes,
Smiles awake you when you rise.
 Sleep, pretty wantons, do not cry,
 And I will sing a lullaby:
Rock them, rock them, lullaby.

Care is heavy, therefore sleep you;
You are care and care must keep you.
 Sleep, pretty wantons, do not cry,
 And I will sing a lullaby:
Rock them, rock them, lullaby.

THOMAS DECKER

Brahms' Lullaby

Lullaby and goodnight,
With lilies of white
And roses of red
To pillow your head:
May you wake when the day
Chases darkness away,
May you wake when the day
Chases darkness away.

Lullaby and goodnight,
Let angels of light
Spread wings round your bed
And guard you from dread.
Slumber gently and deep
In the dreamland of sleep,
Slumber gently and deep
In the dreamland of sleep.

JOHANNES BRAHMS

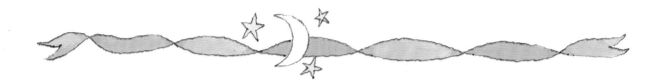

Sleep, baby, sleep.
Thy father guards the sheep;
Thy mother shakes the dreamland tree,
Down falls a little dream for thee;
Sleep, baby, sleep.

Sleep, baby, sleep.
The large stars are the sheep;
The little stars are lambs, I guess,
And the gentle moon is the shepherdess;
Sleep, baby, sleep.

The White Seal's Lullaby

Oh! hush thee, my baby, the night is behind us,
    And black are the waters that sparkled so green.
The moon o'er the combers, looks downward to find us
    At rest in the hollows that rustle between.
Where billow meets billow, then soft be thy pillow;
    Ah, weary wee flipperling, curl at thy ease,
The storm shall not wake thee, nor shark overtake thee,
    Asleep in the arms of the slow-swinging seas.

RUDYARD KIPLING

A Chill

What can lambkins do,
All the keen night through?
Nestle by their woolly mother,
The careful ewe.

What can nestlings do,
In the nightly dew?
Sleep beneath their mother's wing,
Till day breaks anew.

If in field or tree,
There might only be,
Such a warm soft sleeping-place,
Found for me!

CHRISTINA ROSSETTI

Sweet and Low

Sweet and low, sweet and low,
   Wind of the western sea.
Low, low, breathe and blow,
   Wind of the western sea!
   Over the rolling waters go,
   Come from the dying moon,
   and blow,
   Blow him again to me;
While my little one, while my
   pretty one, sleeps.

Sleep and rest, sleep and rest,
   Father will come to thee soon;
Rest, rest, on mother's breast,
   Father will come to thee soon;
   Father will come to his babe
   in the nest,
   Silver sails all out of the west
   Under the silver moon;
Sleep, my little one, my pretty
   one, sleep.

ALFRED, LORD TENNYSON

A Baby's Boat

Baby's boat's a silver moon
Sailing in the sky,
Sailing o'er a sea of sleep
While the stars float by.

Sail, baby, sail
Out upon that sea;
Only don't forget to sail
Back again to me.

Baby's fishing for a dream,
Fishing far and near,
Her line a silver moonbeam is,
Her bait a silver star.

Sail, baby, sail
Out upon that sea;
Only don't forget to sail
Back again to me.

INDEX OF FIRST LINES